OCEAN LIFE UP CLOSE

Jellyfish

by Christina Leaf

BLASTOFF!
3
READERS

BELLWETHER MEDIA · MINNEAPOLIS, MN

Note to Librarians, Teachers, and Parents:

Blastoff! Readers are carefully developed by literacy experts and combine standards-based content with developmentally appropriate text.

Level 1 provides the most support through repetition of high-frequency words, light text, predictable sentence patterns, and strong visual support.

Level 2 offers early readers a bit more challenge through varied simple sentences, increased text load, and less repetition of high-frequency words.

Level 3 advances early-fluent readers toward fluency through increased text and concept load, less reliance on visuals, longer sentences, and more literary language.

Level 4 builds reading stamina by providing more text per page, increased use of punctuation, greater variation in sentence patterns, and increasingly challenging vocabulary.

Level 5 encourages children to move from "learning to read" to "reading to learn" by providing even more text, varied writing styles, and less familiar topics.

Whichever book is right for your reader, Blastoff! Readers are the perfect books to build confidence and encourage a love of reading that will last a lifetime!

This edition first published in 2017 by Bellwether Media, Inc.

No part of this publication may be reproduced in whole or in part without written permission of the publisher. For information regarding permission, write to Bellwether Media, Inc., Attention: Permissions Department, 6012 Blue Circle Dr., Minnetonka, MN 55343.

Library of Congress Cataloging-in-Publication Data

Names: Leaf, Christina.
Title: Jellyfish / by Christina Leaf.
Description: Minneapolis, MN : Bellwether Media, Inc., 2017. | Series: Blastoff! Readers. Ocean Life Up Close | Audience: Ages 5-8. | Audience: Grade K to grade 3. | Includes bibliographical references and index.
Identifiers: LCCN 2015049396 | ISBN 9781626174184 (hardcover : alk. paper)
ISBN 9781618912664 (paperback : alk. paper)
Subjects: LCSH: Jellyfishes–Juvenile literature.
Classification: LCC QL377.S4 L43 2017 | DDC 593.5/3–dc23
LC record available at http://lccn.loc.gov/2015049396

Printed in the United States of America, North Mankato, MN.

Table of Contents

What Are Jellyfish?

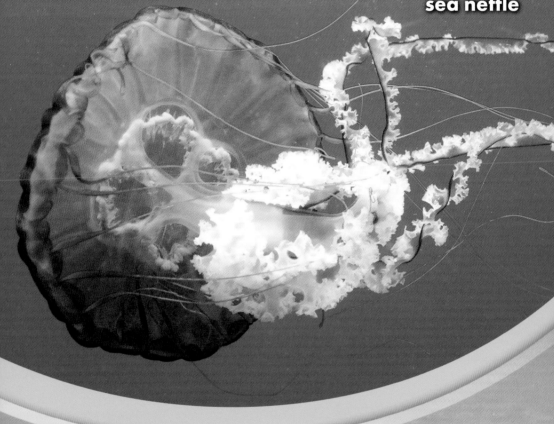

Pacific sea nettle

Jellyfish are a type of **plankton**. They are not actually fish. Some people believe that "jellies" is a better name for them.

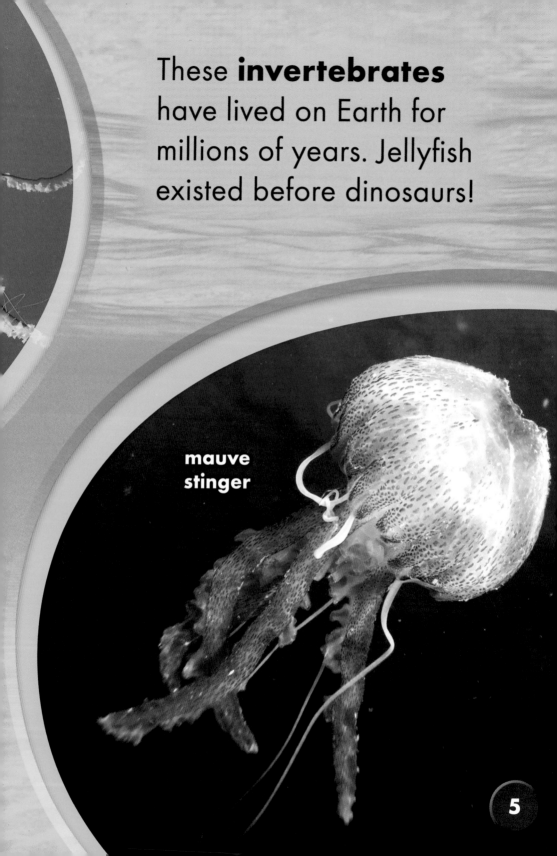

These **invertebrates** have lived on Earth for millions of years. Jellyfish existed before dinosaurs!

mauve stinger

lion's mane
jellyfish

Jellyfish are found all over the
world's oceans. They drift through
open waters.

Many live in shallow coastal waters. But some are in the deepest parts of the ocean!

Species Spotlight
SEA WASP

life span:
less than 1 year

depth range:
0 to 131 feet
(0 to 40 meters)

sea wasp range =

N
W — E
S

conservation status: **least concern**

Extinct	Extinct in the Wild	Critically Endangered	Endangered	Vulnerable	Near Threatened	Least Concern

Truly Jelly?

Water makes up most of a jellyfish's soft, bell-shaped body.

Jellyfish Sizes

Smallest

Eleutheria dichotoma

actual size

0.02 inches
(0.05 centimeters) wide

Largest

lion's mane jellyfish

average human

8 feet
(2.4 meters) wide

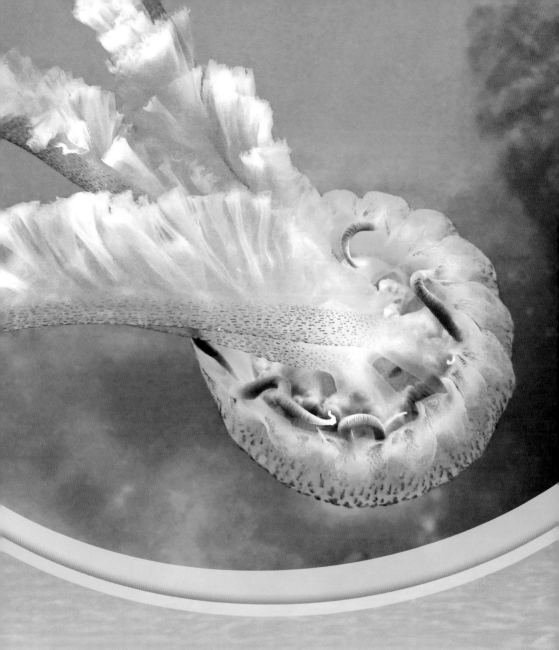

Jellyfish bodies are usually clear.
They easily blend in with water.
Some are brightly colored.

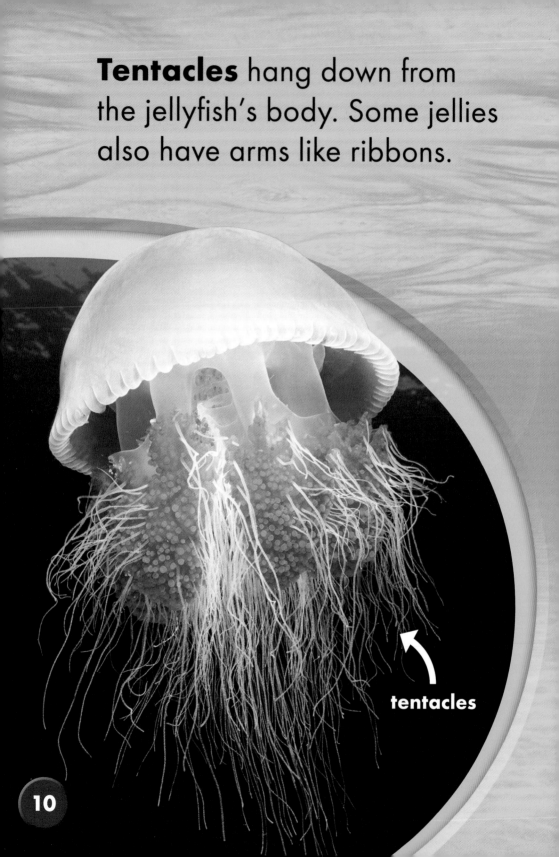

Tentacles hang down from the jellyfish's body. Some jellies also have arms like ribbons.

tentacles

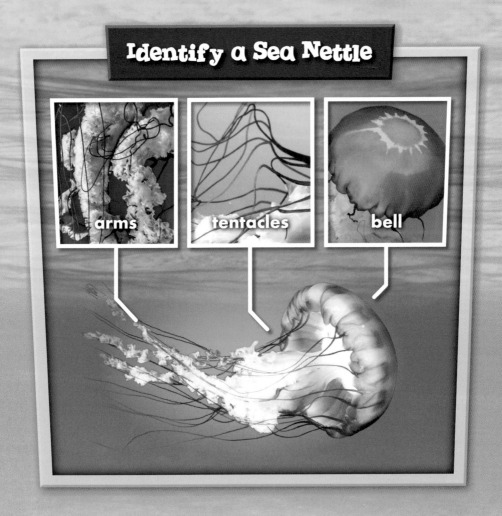

Identify a Sea Nettle

arms

tentacles

bell

Jellyfish do not have bones, blood, or a brain. But some can sense light or smell. Their tentacles can feel animals that touch them.

To swim, jellyfish open and close their bell. They push water out from their body to move forward.

spotted
jellyfish

Jellyfish do not move very fast like this. Most swim little and just float with **currents**.

Jellies hunt as they drift. The **carnivores** eat other plankton, such as tiny crabs and fish.

Their trailing tentacles brush against **prey** and sting them with **venom**. Then the food is brought up to the mouth inside the bell.

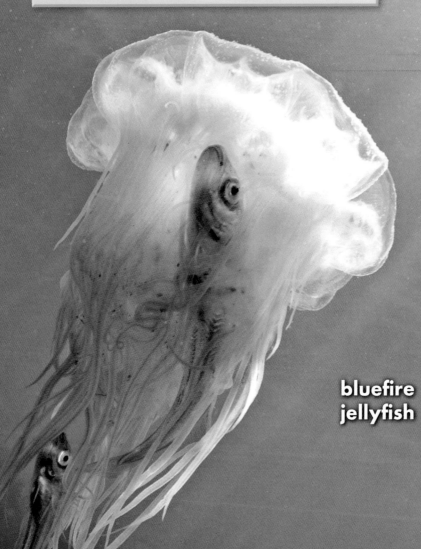

plankton

mosquito larvae

bluefire jellyfish

15

Sea Enemies

blue rockfish

leatherback sea turtles

ocean sunfish

green sea turtle

mosaic jellyfish

Few animals want to eat jellyfish because of their sting. However, jellyfish venom does not harm every **predator**.

Jellies are a treat for some fish. Sea turtles also love snacking on them.

rabbitfish

Coming into Bloom

Jellyfish begin as eggs. They turn into **larvae** and drift to the ocean floor. There, they attach to a rock or solid place.

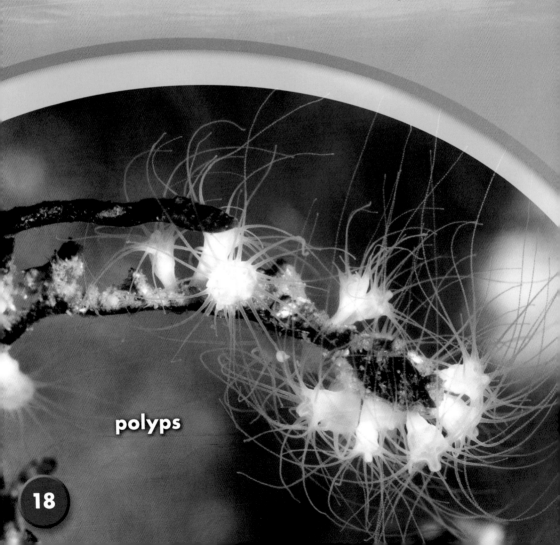

polyps

Life Cycle of a Jellyfish

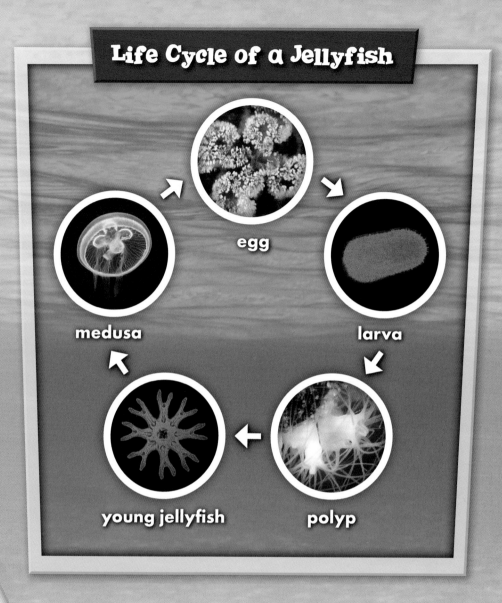

egg

larva

medusa

polyp

young jellyfish

Polyps grow from the larvae. A polyp breaks off layers that become young jellyfish. These change into **medusas**.

moon
jellyfish

Medusas drift off into the
ocean. Currents push the jellies
into groups called **swarms**.

Seasonal **blooms** bring even more jellyfish together. Thousands may collect in bays or coastal waters!

golden jellyfish

Glossary

blooms—large groups of jellyfish that form in small spaces; jellyfish blooms happen for a short amount of time, often with the seasons.

carnivores—animals that only eat meat

currents—patterns of water movement in an ocean

invertebrates—animals without a backbone

larvae—early, tiny forms of an animal that must go through a big change to become adults

medusas—adult jellyfish

plankton—ocean plants or animals that drift in water; most plankton are tiny.

polyps—animals that have tube-shaped bodies and are attached to a hard place; jellyfish are polyps for part of their life cycle.

predator—an animal that hunts other animals for food

prey—animals that are hunted by other animals for food

swarms—groups of jellyfish

tentacles—long, bendable parts of a jellyfish that are attached to the body

venom—a poison a jellyfish makes

To Learn More

AT THE LIBRARY
Magby, Meryl. *Jellyfish*. New York, N.Y.: PowerKids Press, 2013.

Raum, Elizabeth. *Box Jellyfish*. Mankato, Minn.: Amicus High Interest, 2016.

Roza, Greg. *Jellyfish*. New York, N.Y.: Gareth Stevens Publishing, 2016.

ON THE WEB
Learning more about jellyfish is as easy as 1, 2, 3.

1. Go to www.factsurfer.com.

2. Enter "jellyfish" into the search box.

3. Click the "Surf" button and you will see a list of related web sites.

With factsurfer.com, finding more information is just a click away.

Index

The images in this book are reproduced through the courtesy of: Edwin Verin, front cover (left, right); Lee Yiu Tung, front cover (center), p. 3; Norman Chan, p. 4; Tiago Sa Brito, p. 5; Joost van Uffelen, p. 6; Ron and Valerie Taylor/ ardea.c / Pantheon/ SuperStock, p. 7; Vilainecrevette, pp. 9, 13; SuperStock/ Glow Images, p. 10; Richard A McMillin, p. 11 (top left); Pavel Vakhrushev, p. 11 (top center, bottom); Steve Lagreca, p. 11 (top right); Chai Seamaker, p. 12; Lebendkulturen.de, p. 15 (top left); Smith1972, p. 15 (top right); WaterFrame/ Alamy, p. 15 (bottom); Stan Shebs/ Wikipedia, p. 16 (top left); Stephanie Rousseau, p. 16 (top center); Kristina Vackova, p. 16 (top right); Rich Carey, pp. 16 (bottom), 17; blickwinkel/ Alamy, pp. 18, 19 (bottom right); NHPA/ SuperStock, p. 19 (top); Vladimir Wrangel, p. 19 (center left); Biodisc/ Visuals Unlimited/ Corbis, p. 19 (center right); Carolina Biological/ Visuals Unlimited/ Corbis, p. 19 (bottom left); A_Lesik, p. 20; Mohamed AlQubaisi, p. 21.